The Soul of a Poet

By: Stephan Willea

This book is dedicated to the wonderful woman who will one day steal the key to my heart, and be the one and only love of my life.

I would like to thank (you) the buyer for purchasing my book. With every copy sold there is more love, compassion and hope to get past the tough times in life.

I would also like to thank my family and friends for supporting me through the process of writing this work.

Table of Contents

<u>True Love</u>

What is True Love you might be
asking…

How do you know if you have found
Love Everlasting…

It's hard to know but if you'd allow…

Lots of it has to do with not the why
but how…

It's not why you do the things you
do…

Do it all wrong and it will go all
askew…

Love is dealing with someone's
mistakes…

It does not matter how long it may
take…

Can you sit back and let them make
a blunder...

Even if there whole world gets torn
asunder...

Will you be there to pick the pieces
up...

Just like your prized shattered
teacup...

And will you be able to do it gently...

And put it back together correctly...

You have to watch them weather
the storm...

Even if they become all shattered
and torn...

Will you be with them through the
tears...

Consoling them through all their
greatest fears...

If you can do all th's than True Love you must have…

For these things do not come in halves…

I've said before and I'll say it again now…

True Love is not known by the why…..BUT HOW!!!

◊◊◊◊◊◊◊◊◊◊◊◊◊◊◊◊◊◊◊◊◊◊◊◊◊◊◊◊◊◊◊◊◊◊◊◊◊◊◊

Angel of my Eyes

I'd like to know when cometh the day...

When everyone will stop leading me astray...

For what I seek is not very hard...

Just one women without a charade...

One and only one is all I need...

And if I could find her she'd be filled with beauty...

Beauty can come in many forms...

Even from those who have weathered storms...

For beauty is in the eye of the
beholder...

But seems harder to find as I get
older...

So still today I look toward the skys...

Till I find the Angel of my Eyes...

◊◊◊◊◊◊◊◊◊◊◊◊◊◊◊◊◊◊◊◊◊◊◊◊◊◊◊◊◊◊◊◊◊◊◊◊◊

Finding Truth

Futures will come and pasts will go...

All you ask is the willingness to
grow...

To look inward to ones deepest
thoughts...

And try to connect your own life's
dots...

You ask yourself all your questions...

But don't listen to anyone's
suggestions...

It's time to find out what others
know...

Because many are willing to help
you grow...

You hold yourself back for many things…

It's time to let go and sprout your wings…

It's time to fly away from things most foul…

And it's time to let out your biggest howl…

For there is still yet a distance to travel…

So don't let your feet get caught in the gravel…

You must push forward to reach your goal…

To find out what's really inside your soul…

Keep searching till you have a smile most radiant…

And don't get set back by worldly events…

The world is not what makes you …

And anyone who says so has no clue…

For you will make your biggest triumph…

When you cut out the worlds defiance…

Positive thinking will help you out…

And true happiness will crush all doubt…

Fight back the negative is what you must do…

Tell all the hatred that you're through…

For every day you have peace of
mind...

Your greatest attributes are
defined...

You will become who you are meant
to be...

When you throw away all that
debris...

Build up a soul that is so beautiful...

With self-love that is so bountiful...

Loving yourself is step number one...

Once this happens you can love
anyone...

For having a mind with a beautiful
state...

Will help you find your real soul
mate...

Be true to yourself and you will find...

Your happiness is no longer
confined...

And once all the hatred has been
overrun...

You can finally say..... I have won...

◊◊◊◊◊◊◊◊◊◊◊◊◊◊◊◊◊◊◊◊◊◊◊◊◊◊◊◊◊◊◊◊◊◊◊

<u>Dove</u>

I have nothing but memories of a
once happy life...

As I think of the one that could have
been my wife...

All she gave was smiles and love...

You could say she was my dove...

Her personality was as bright as
rainbows and sunshine...

And her love was as intoxicating as a
glass of red wine...

Her laugh was beautiful and
unique...

And her charm held a special
Mystique...

Her smile brightened my darkest days...

And smashed all doubt that was in my way...

She encouraged me to be my best...

Even when I was put to the test...

She stood by me through thick and thin...

Even as I fought my demons from within...

But I was stubborn and I wouldn't see...

That I was pushing her away from me...

She gave me love but I did not return...

And now I know it's what she yearned...

I have changed and wish to see...

The one I love return to me...

I messed up this I know...

But if she'd come back I'd surely
glow...

All I wish is for my dove ...

To understand she still has my love...

◊◊◊◊◊◊◊◊◊◊◊◊◊◊◊◊◊◊◊◊◊◊◊◊◊◊◊◊◊◊◊◊◊◊◊◊◊

Best of Me

My Heart gets played like a well-

tuned Violin...

While I try not to share the pain from

within...

People say Love comes and goes...

But i say to Hell with Those...

For I know who still has my Heart...

Even though she and I are now

apart...

I still hope one day she will see...

That I now show the best of me...

I have long been not myself...

While I gazed out from upon the

shelf...

And now I have learned...

That your Love can be easily

turned...

I wish what I have learned I could

show...

But there is no way for me to know...

I still sit and I still hope...

That my true feelings will be looked

at from under a microscope...

For than everyone will see...

The one I love still holds the Best of

Me!!!

Broken Hearted Birthday Poem

Congratulations on getting another year older...

I hope your mood will never again be colder...

Even though we are now apart...

I want you to know you'll always have my Heart...

I know you can't believe you're older by another year...

Even though I wish you were still here...

Just know I'm happy to say...

I still wish you a WONDERFUL BIRTHDAY!

◊◊◊◊◊◊◊◊◊◊◊◊◊◊◊◊◊◊◊◊◊◊◊◊◊◊◊◊◊◊◊◊◊◊◊◊◊◊

Cupcake

Small, Adorable, Cute, Intoxicating,
Amazing, Addictive, Beautiful, Full of
Energy and Love,

Possibly Deadly.

<u>Cupcake's Poem</u>

You are a cupcake can't you see...

That you still hold the best of me...

You may feel very small...

But to me your soul still calls...

You may be adorable and cute...

This no one can dispute...

Your energy is intoxicating lifting me
to the skies...

Even though you hide behind your
disguise...

You always had my Eyes gazing...

Because you are so amazing...

Your personality is beautiful and addictive ...

While your soul has always been mystic...

Full of energy you have always been...

Like the sounds from a beautiful violin...

You may be deadly if provoked...

As I have always joked...

Even though my heart still aches...

This is how I describe you cupcake...

◊◊◊◊◊◊◊◊◊◊◊◊◊◊◊◊◊◊◊◊◊◊◊◊◊◊◊◊◊◊◊◊◊◊◊◊◊

Moon and Skies

A moonless night and darkened skies...

Are all that lie before my eyes...

It doesn't matter what I do...

I just rekindle my love for you...

Moving on is harder than one might think...

As one can now read from my minds ink...

My thoughts and worry are what causes me torment...

As it's hard to make true loves feelings dormant...

Our souls will be forever bound...

Even through hollow battlegrounds...

Maybe one day our paths will
reconverge...

To once again never diverge...

For I would like a moon filled night
with starry skies...

To be laid out before my eyes!!!

◊◊◊◊◊◊◊◊◊◊◊◊◊◊◊◊◊◊:◊◊◊◊◊◊◊◊◊◊◊◊◊◊◊

My Fears

I have learned by now when she
suffers pain...

I feel the same within my brain...

While she gets targeted and
attacked...

I sit here with my heart still cracked...

I continue to tell her I'll be here...

But I worry I venture to near...

Wait till she calls me she has said...

But staying away causes my heart
dread...

I do my best to keep my distance...

But I worry she'll forget of my
existence...

I fear while she deals with it all…

She is headed nowhere but the fall…

For her feelings I am scared…

Because I feel she's unprepared…

She is hurt this I can see…

For I fear her emotions are headed
for the black sea…

For her mind I wish to save…

And to keep her heart from the
grave…

For the beach is where ill stand…

While I still wait for her hand…

To rescue her is my wish…

Even though I know it's selfish…

For here I wait to see...

If again she'll ever trust me...

As I sit here and try to cope...

All I still have is hope...

My Mind

When we had split...

There were things she said not to quit...

There were feelings shared...

Ones I thought would never be dared...

Get yourself help is what she said...

Even though I thought I'd rather be Dead...

But help I did receive ...

And learned things that before I would not believe...

I have now become a better Man...

I no longer consider myself a Madman...

Now I aim to give what I received...

To those that now have pain and grieve...

But now all I see is her suffer...

And I know she's been through things much tougher...

And now I try to help her believe...

That there is more for her to receive...

Even still I hope she finds...

That she is still all that runs through my mind!!!

◊◊◊◊◊◊◊◊◊◊◊◊◊◊◊◊◊◊◊◊◊◊◊◊◊◊◊◊◊◊◊◊◊◊◊◊

Rise

You may think your world has ended...

When your love gets suspended...

You say to yourself that you're alone...

Stuck inside your shattered home...

You blame yourself for it all...

Trying to wash it down with alcohol...

I'm here to help if you'd allow...

Let me give you my thoughts for chow...

You're not alone in your strife...

So will you please put down the knife...

For we all have demons we must fight...

And we all have things that cause us fright...

Hurt and breakups happen to us all...

And we have all headed for the fall...

Take a moment so you can find...

The pieces of your shattered mind...

Build yourself up to be stronger...

And the pain won't be with you any longer...

Find what makes you who you are...

Even the fun and the bizarre...

It's the little quirks that make us outstanding...

These prove that we are self-commanding...

Even in your coldest December...

You must sit back and remember...

No matter how good you were back then...

You'll find you've become a better person...

For knowledge is the key to strength...

With stuff one learns by yearly length...

And without this insight you will find...

You will be left far behind...

To be sure this does not happen...

You need to be your own life's captain...

Live your life with positive emotions...

And you will not drown in the oceans...

Live day to day with no strife...

And you will have a better life...

Better for you and better for all...

That you have now risen from your downfall...

◊◊◊◊◊◊◊◊◊◊◊◊◊◊◊◊◊◊◊◊◊◊◊◊◊◊◊◊◊◊◊◊◊◊◊◊

Poems of a Lost Love

I

When the Void in your Heart has
become so Deep...

You find yourself unable to sleep...

But before the Darkness turns to
Dawn...

One must find the place where One
Belongs...

II

I look over seas of Oceans Blue...

And find Myself Still Thinking of you...

I know the water is very Cold...

Yet I still hope one day my Heart will
be Whole...

III

When I look up and the sky is Dark
and Gray...

I think to Myself, This could be my
Final Day...

But when the sky clears I will see...

There is Still so much more left for
me...

Sit and Wait

Your smile was as fresh as a
springtime flower

That I loved to see in my Waking
hour

You brought Joy and Love into my
life

Making me believe there was no
such thing as strife

All of space and time was laid
before us

Yet there was nothing that seemed
that dangerous

But little by little we let ourselves be
torn away

And eventually we went astray

While others wanted to point at one
for fault

All we wanted was to make the lies
Halt

For the lies bred nothing but anguish

But it all could have stopped with
peaceful language

In the end the flower had withered

And my heart was locked in the
eternal blizzard

For while they saw that you were
suffering

No one cared about my emotions
buffering

So while others tried again to make
the flower sprout

I stood there and got locked out

Everyone reached to give you help

While they wished for me to yelp

Never once did I point the finger at
you with blame

But it seems that was where all others
were aimed

Still I wish for peace for us

No longer with any of the fuss

If people ask me how I cope

All I say is "I have hope"

While I wished we were together for
years of at least eight

I guess I will stay here and ..... Sit and
Wait...

◊◊◊◊◊◊◊◊◊◊◊◊◊◊◊◊◊◊◊◊◊◊◊◊◊◊◊◊◊◊◊◊◊◊◊◊

The Mountain

I'm standing here at the bottom...

Looking up at the mountain...

This huge obstacle that lies before
my path...

I feel as though I've been struck by
heavens wrath...

I continue to push to better myself...

To get out from behind this bitter
shelf...

My feelings have put me in a deep
blockade...

And my emotions have sent me all
astray...

Farther and farther into the
blackness...

I feel as though I have dived into
madness...

While there are many who sit and stare...

The pain gets harder and harder to bare...

The pain could all be lifted...

And all my emotions shifted...

If the one that causes the pain...

Would help me see if I am still sane...

It would not be difficult to make my heart unlock...

All we'd have to do..... is talk...

Open up about what we used to be...

And start up a conversation .... with me...

Talking it out would be step number one...

Continue from there and we could see the healing done...

When the healing gets finished...

My pain will be diminished...

And then the world will see...

I'll be once again free to be ....me...

◊◊◊◊◊◊◊◊◊◊◊◊◊◊◊◊◊◊◊◊◊◊◊◊◊◊◊◊◊◊◊◊◊◊◊◊

The Pain of my heart

While people say the sky will clear...

I sit back and fight the tears...

For my heart that continues to
break...

Is the reason that everything still
aches...

Every day I fight the pain...

That still is hanging in my brain...

I wish my heart to be unbroken...

But still there's things that are not
spoken...

While the silence has been
devastating...

Into the sorrows my heart goes
cascading...

I feel there's a never-ending drought...

And I still can't find my way back out...

I wish there'd come a storm...

That would bring torrents that swarm...

To put out my heart's desires...

That still burn like wildfires...

For my feelings crash and burn...

And bring to me some concern...

There are things that make me sacred...

Many I fear will be shared...

One can consider a piece of art...

Is the pain I hide in my heart...

◊◊◊◊◊◊◊◊◊◊◊◊◊◊◊◊◊◊◊◊◊◊◊◊◊◊◊◊◊◊◊◊◊◊◊◊◊

<u>Truth</u>

It may be hard when you're left in
the dark...

Because somebody has broken your
heart...

You thought you had the love you
wanted...

But now you're alone and your
minds all haunted...

But moving on is what you must do...

Because they no longer care for
you...

Do not believe in your minds lies...

For even good things come in
disguise...

You may feel that you're all alone...

Even lock yourself in your home...

But if you'd open the windows to your heart...

Your eyes will see the darkness fall apart..

For feeling come and feelings go...

But true love is something to behold...

True love is something you will find...

And it all starts within your mind...

For people see what can be...

When you share with them your hearts key...

Share your love with others you may find...

And you may see that you are not so blind...

You thought you were blind to the ways of the heart...

But now you know everyone has played there part...

To help you become a better you...

And now it's your soul you look into...

Where you will find the thing most beautiful...

Is the one thing that will not be beatable...

For the one thing you will find...

Is that you yourself are one of a kind...

And if others try to change your mind...

You can tell them that they are blind...

For you have grown and you are strong...

And you have learned it's the world that's wrong...

Be yourself that's all that matters...

And you will shush all the chatters...

For you have learned with all you see...

There is no better way to be...

◊◊◊◊◊◊◊◊◊◊◊◊◊◊◊◊◊◊◊◊◊◊◊◊◊◊◊◊◊◊◊◊◊◊

Lessons Learned

There once was a time when I
thought I had it all...

And I never once dreamed that I
could ever fall...

I had my head in the clouds way to
long...

And I thought I controlled the world's
song...

I was high and mighty beating on
my chest...

And I never thought my pride would
be put to the test...

But I was too full of myself and I have
found...

That my pride is what got buried in
the ground...

For it's not pride that matters the most...

This I have found from my observation post...

Looking inward for what matters most...

Searching my soul from coast to coast...

I have found its time to enjoy the little things...

To enjoy my life and what it brings...

My life may not be perfect by any means...

It's like I'm getting tested for new vaccines...

But the incredible lessons that I have learned...

Are from life's trials that I have overturned...

Some are obstacles no one should
ever face...

But I have found them running after
the chase...

I've spent too much time pursuing
useless things...

And not enough for what life's
happiest moments would bring...

Focus on the happy thoughts is what
I should do...

Even the little ones will help get me
through...

For the little thoughts will bring ones
much bigger...

And those are the ones that will fill
me with vigor...

To be healthy with the thoughts of
my own mind...

And to have peace so I will find...

That my mind and soul are bound as one...

And now True Happiness has begun...

I have finally cut the binding strings...

And found happiness with life and all that it brings...

◊◊◊◊◊◊◊◊◊◊◊◊◊◊◊◊◊◊◊◊◊◊◊◊◊◊◊◊◊◊◊◊◊◊◊◊◊◊

Don't give up

Have you fallen on times of hard...

And completely lost your guard...

Does your whole world seem like it's
ended...

And your galaxy has been
suspended...

Have you decided to throw in the
towel...

And never again attempt to howl...

Well I am here for you my friend...

To tell you why the good doesn't
have to end...

Times may have been rough this is
true...

But there are plenty of reasons you
can pull through...

When you open your eyes and see the sun...

Remember that a new day has just begun...

A new day to wash away the pain of the old...

And give you something new to behold...

No matter the pain you may be going through...

There is still someone who has love for you...

Be it an animal or a family member...

Someone will help you through your coldest December...

And someday soon, could be tomorrow...

The sun will come out and melt your sorrows...

And just like the great skies above…

You will once again find your love…

Love is a mystery this is true…

But it all comes from your point of view…

To find the things you most desire…

You have to have the thoughts of love prior…

You never know where love may be hiding…

Or what your path has been deciding…

But I can tell you this, my friend…

Good things always come…… in the end…

◊◊

What I search for

As I walk through this life of mine...

I search for the one who will make me shine...

I search from sea to sea...

To find the one that's best for me...

What I ask for is not much...

Just a love with a soft touch...

She must be beautiful in her own way...

And offer a love that will never decay...

She needs to have a mind most kind...

And have her best attributes defined...

Loving and caring in every respect...

And be her own life's architect...

She needs to be my guiding light...

For when I want to give up the fight...

She needs to be able to share her pain...

So she can see she's not insane...

Our love will travel in both directions...

And we will give each other corrections...

I will be her sturdy wall...

To keep her from her own downfall...

I will give her a love that's profound...

And our souls will be forever bound...

For love has to be shared between two people...

Who continue to see each other as equals...

One woman for me is all I ask...

That does not hide behind a mask...

She will be a woman of beauty...

And not a single bit snooty...

For she will have a heart of gold...

That will be something to behold...

So I'll keep searching till I find...

A beautiful woman with a beautiful mind...

◇◇◇◇◇◇◇◇◇◇◇◇◇◇◇◇◇◇◇◇◇◇◇◇◇◇◇◇◇◇◇◇◇◇◇◇

Two Hearts

I wait but she doesn't show...

I want but she doesn't know...

I love but she doesn't care...

Sadly I will not always be there...

For one can only wait so long...

Before its time to move on...

I cannot wait forever...

So now I chose to dissever...

For I have waited long enough...

And my heart has been left with a
scuff...

But I have chosen to move on...

Till my heart finds a new dawn...

For the heart yearns to find its
mate...

And a time and a cause to
celebrate...

For when two hearts to each other
have spoken...

There bond will remain unbroken...

So as two hearts take a raft
downstream...

True love continues to reign
supreme...

Two hearts with love in tow...

And two souls that are bound will
glow...

For they have found the only one...

That cannot be replaced by
anyone...

As they sit and watch the waterfall…

They will know True Love…. Has conquered all…

◊◊

The Pull of Granite Eyes

As I look into eyes of darken brown...

I can't think of anything more
profound...

The feelings I have for you are
known...

To be as hard as granite stone...

Mountains will grow from our love...

And pierce the great skies above...

The earthen clay is ours to mold...

And make the most beautiful things
to behold...

As water falls from granite cliffs...

We will think of all our gifts...

And as we canoe down the river
stream...

We will have plenty of time to dream...

As one day our kids will romp and play...

And you will have another birthday...

As I look at you as our loves brand new...

I will say....... I Love You...

◊◊◊◊◊◊◊◊◊◊◊◊◊◊◊◊◊◊◊◊◊◊◊◊◊◊◊◊◊◊◊◊◊◊◊◊◊◊

<u>The Beauty of Evergreen Eyes</u>

As I look into eyes of natures green...

Never have I felt so serine...

As I visit fields of evergreen flowers...

I can't help but ask for springtime showers...

As I watch this worlds big movie screen...

I search for the most vibrant pastures I've ever seen...

Fields of beauty where we can run...

And the little ones can have some fun...

And as we watch the amazing view...

I will say......... I Love You...

The Lure of Ocean Eyes

As I look into Eyes of deepest blue...

I find out how I feel for you...

You take my skies of stormy sorrow...

And turn them into a better
tomorrow...

You take my seas of ocean blue...

And guide the ship of love straight
through...

And through all the fears and stormy
tears...

We'll find some of our best years...

As our children play in shallow
streams...

We'll think back on all our dreams...

And find that the sun will shine with a
radiant glow...

And bring out the most beautiful
rainbow...

And as certain as the springtime
morning dew...

I have to say......... i Love You...

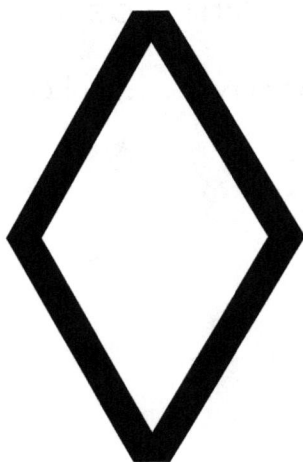